Destined
Overcoming Shame and Defeat

Tamika A. Marable

T.A.L.K. Publishing
5215 North Ironwood Road, Suite 200
Glendale, WI 53217
talkconsulting.net

T.A.L.K.
Publishing
TELL.ACCEPT.LEARN.KNOW.
talkconsulting.net

Title: Destined
Subtitle: Overcoming Shame and Defeat
ISBN: 978-1-952327-23-0

Dedication

To all the women who have been an inspiration and helped me develop into the woman I am today, I dedicate this book. Your kindness, generosity, and love mean more to me than I could ever express in words. I'm confident that each of you knows who you are. I love and appreciate you so very much!

To my sisters Jensine and Jereba and my aunts Ifama and Anita who are no longer with us, you all are genuinely missed and deeply loved.

Finally, to my foster mother, Ms. Beverly Wilson, who is no longer with us physically, your dedication to children and families left an imprint on my heart, and I will always hold a special place for you there too.

Destined to Be

A mirror reflects what stands before it. When I look in the mirror, what do I see? I see me, of course—pretty, smart, and happy as can be. As I continue looking, I begin to wonder, *What do you see when you look at me?*

Disappointing memories involving my mother surface to discourage me. Degrading words from men appear to shame me. Hurtful words from my "friends" emerge to taunt me. Negative comments enemies have said beam back at me. Unexpected words heard from my father embarrass me. These words create another image that stares right back at me!

I blush in shame. Could this be what they all see?

Possibly.

But as I look in the mirror, I must reflect upon what I see—who I'm destined to be.

Preface

Have you ever thought about destiny and wanted it to have its perfect way with you? I can confidently say that many of us take our destinies for granted. We rarely think about destiny until we feel its gentle touch tapping us on the shoulder, saying, Are you willing to go where I want to take you? Life's circumstances can at times leave us questioning not only our decisions but our entire existence.

One day, I found myself sitting in my car reflecting on the divorce I had just finalized and feeling ashamed. As I thought back over my life leading up to that moment, I felt discouraged. I can remember thinking, What am I going to do now? My son was about three years old and would now be living without both his parents raising him together. This thought saddened me because my decision to get married had been built upon avoiding that exact situation. Thinking back, I realized that dealing with shame, loss, grief, and defeat had become the story of my life. I wondered why my relationships were failing. I felt emotionally unstable, and I thought I had no one to trust.

In 2010, I began writing the story of what I would call my life; I had it all mapped out, the details, the story line, and the objective. However, there seemed to be another plan awaiting me. One day I rushed into the house with intentions of coming right back out, but it took me a while. When I returned, someone had broken into my car. My glove compartment was wide open with everything in disarray. My wallet was there, but the money inside was gone. My head hung low as I glared toward the back seat. My backpack was stolen too. I shouted with fury as I realized my driver's license, credit cards, taxes, social security card, and the manuscript were all gone.

In that instance, the idea of me writing a book was stolen too. I had bigger fish to fry because I was feeling defeated yet again. I needed to work through my emotions because I became suspicious of everyone around me, not knowing who to trust. It's now about ten years since that happened, and I am writing with a new perspective, a new concept, and an entirely different purpose.

I now know God had a plan too! While you read this book, your life will never be the same. After you finish this book, you will be accepting of a change. The Bible tells us,

"Do not be conformed to this world but be transformed by the renewal of your mind, that by testing you may discern what the will of God is, what is good and acceptable and perfect" (The Holy Bible, English Standard Version, 2001, Romans 12:2).

Contents

Introduction 13

It All Starts Somewhere 15

Somebody, Please Step In! 21

The Cycle Continues 27

Tragedy Strikes 33

Enough Is Enough 41

Father, Can You Hear Me? 51

Wait for Love 59

Redefined Life 67

Defining Yourself through Purpose 73

Fruit of the Spirit: Poems 79

Shame-Less 83

Destiny 85

Journal Your Progress/Process 87

Introduction

I often speak of shame throughout this book; therefore, it's crucial to know what it is. Shame is a painful feeling of humiliation or distress caused by the consciousness of wrong or foolish behavior. Shame is also defined as a feeling of guilt, regret, or sadness because you know you have done something wrong.

Psychologists suggest that feelings of shame are associated with low self-esteem, hostility, and psychological distress. These feelings are often triggered by social events that resulted in a change in personal status or where feelings of rejection are perceived. Shame also involves a sense of inferiority, hopelessness, helplessness, and a desire to hide personal flaws.

As I journey through past experiences with twenty-twenty vision, seeing things a bit clearer now, the process of writing this book gives me hope, courage, and peace. I experience a subtle knowing that God connected you as the reader and me as the writer for a specific reason. In past times I would write to God and ask him to use me to help children and families, to be a connector and an example to encourage others. This book is one way God has answered those prayers.

Stepping out on faith to do what God is calling and positioning you to do, although scary at times, must be your priority. Right now, you may not see what the end looks like for you, but as you continue to seek God's will for your life, ultimately, it will be revealed.

At the beginning of each chapter, I provide statistics from the United States Census Bureau that are related to the life experience I share. I also share letters to God, then a reflection I call "Twenty-Twenty Vision." Many of the experiences I share are ones some people find themselves dealing with today. God's message for me during this journey was that I didn't have to live with the shame of being or becoming a statistic. My message to you is, neither do you.

> Do not fret or have any anxiety about anything, but in every circumstance and in everything, by prayer and petition (definite requests), with thanksgiving, continue to make your wants known to God. (Amplified Bible, Classic Edition, 1954/1987, Philippians 4:6)

It All Starts Somewhere

- One in nine girls under the age of eighteen experience sexual abuse or assault at an adult's hands.
- Twenty percent of sexual assault victims are under eight years of age.
- Thirty percent of sexual assaults are not reported, and ninety-three percent of the perpetrators are known to the victim.

My mother had five girls to raise on her own. Growing up, my sisters and I didn't always live together. My older sister and I lived with my aunt in Chicago, two other sisters lived with another aunt, and my mother had the youngest with her. Although most of my childhood before age seven is a blur, I recall a conversation between my mother and my aunt when I was about six. During this conversation, my mother made it clear that she wanted to take us with her to live in Milwaukee. The conversation seemed hostile, and I could tell my aunt was upset. The last words I heard from that conversation was "Come get your damn kids, then." I was sad when I heard her say those words. I was thinking, *What happened and why do we have to leave?*

I can't remember the time frame between that conversation and the moment we were in the back seat of my mother's car, on our way to Milwaukee. I was excited and nervous at the same time. I was happy to be with my mother but scared of what would happen in an unfamiliar place.

I can remember living near Thirty-eighth and Brown in a yellow duplex; we stayed in the lower level. Things seemed to be going well. My sister and I shared a room with bunk beds. I was afraid to sleep on the top bunk, so she let me have the bottom. Having the bottom bunk made more sense to me because I was younger than her. My mother talked about getting our other sisters to live with us, but they hadn't come yet. Around this time, my youngest sister was about two months old. I loved playing with her as if she were a doll. She was so cute. She had the prettiest caramel-tone complexion and a head full of curly black hair.

Not long after we began staying in this house, we met our mother's new boyfriend. He was nice. He would watch us when our mother was asleep or not at home. Together we would watch television and sometimes watch him rough play with his son when he came over. He would buy food for us, and I can remember my sister trying to cook dinner often around this time, which was slightly different because she was nine. One could say that things were changing a lot as time went on.

It was late at night and the house was dark when I heard footsteps and saw the light coming from underneath the bathroom door. I squeezed my eyes shut as I attempted to pretend that I was sleeping. My heart raced as I began to tuck the edges of the blanket under the sides of my body. *Please don't let him come in here tonight.*

Immediately after that thought, I could feel his presence standing over me, and it didn't matter how tight I tried to keep that blanket tucked. I felt it being pulled from under me slowly but surely. Something smooth, like skin, glided across my lips.

What is that? I kept telling myself, *Whatever you do, don't open your eyes.*

The curiosity wouldn't let me keep my eyes closed. I squinted with my eyes partly open, and I saw him. I couldn't believe it was my mother's boyfriend. I was scared and thought, *Don't move, keep quiet, and maybe this will be over soon.*

The next morning, I woke up wondering if what I experienced was a dream. *Did that happen?* I rationalized within my seven-year-old self. I thought back to the dreadful moment, remembering small details like his hands rubbing across my body. First, my legs, then my private parts. I don't recall exactly everything that happened that night, but I remember feeling uncomfortable around my mother's boyfriend after that. The feelings of discomfort didn't matter because he wasn't going anywhere. I didn't understand what made me keep quiet about it then. Today, I believe the answer is that I was carrying shame.

Although he never threatened me or told me not to say anything, I was ashamed to admit that what happened had occurred. I knew something was wrong with this situation but couldn't articulate if it was my fault. What made matters worse is that he walked around as if it didn't happen. I decided to forget about it, erase it from my mind, never to be spoken of again.

It wasn't until I was about thirty that I told my mother about this experience. When I did, she broke down in tears. She was devastated and asked me why I didn't tell her sooner. My response was, "I don't know why."

After hearing her reaction, I was surprised because I had always lacked a certain level of trust toward my mother. However, at that moment, I felt like she cared and possibly would have done something had I told her then.

Letters to God

WHAT ARE THE DESIRES OF YOUR HEART?
Sunday, 10/10/2004, 9:37 p.m.

Dear Lord,

Thank you for all you've done for me. I know sometimes I might not show it, but I am incredibly grateful. Today you spoke to my spirit and asked, When are you going to become the woman I have called you to be?

The answer is, I'm ready, but Lord, I need you to give me the courage and the strength to step out on faith and begin to get things done. Lord, you know my heart, so I pray that you fulfill all my heart's desires if it's in your will. If you have a vision for me, I hope and pray that you would reveal it to me. I have decided that I want to worship you in spirit and truth. Please give me the will to learn of you and seek you to become a better person and a role model for others so that when they look at me, they would see Jesus in me and not wonder if I know the Lord. Lord, I know you brought me a long way, and without these experiences, I would not know the things I know now. Lord, I pray that you continue to reveal yourself to me.

A PRAYER FOR YOU
Tuesday, 11/10/2020, 9:30 p.m.

Dear Lord,

I pray for all young girls who currently face or will face the challenges of being sexually abused. Lord, I pray that you will step in by sending someone who will remove them from that situation. I pray that the truth is revealed to all who need to know.
I pray that peace and love will manifest within the young girl's heart, and she will see that it's not her fault. I pray she will recognize your presence in her life. Lord give her the strength to tell someone she trusts.

Lord, give the person that she confides in the courage to take the appropriate actions to ensure she is safe, and please remove any doubt or shame they each may face.

I pray that the perpetrator feels a sense of conviction about their actions and seeks the required help.

Twenty-Twenty Vision

As I reflect upon the prayer from 2004, I see myself growing in maturity toward the Lord. I was willing to lay my life down for what was best for the kingdom. I desired to use my life as an example and an encouragement for God's people. I sought to know God's will for my life instead of focusing on my own, and I hoped for the two to align. The Word tells us that God will give us the desires of our hearts. However, there is a stipulation—we must delight ourselves in the Lord. Delight means to please greatly. God requires this of us. To please God, we must first have a relationship with him. A relationship with God is not as hard as many may assume. Being obedient to the Holy Spirit's convictions and living a life that includes God's wisdom is a start. Reading our Word should not be something we feel obligated to do but instead are happy we get to do.

I went to God with a thankful heart, which is essential to living a life of purpose. Having a grateful heart offers us the opportunity to show love and receive love too. It helps us find contentment in the good times and not-so-good times because we know that seasons change eventually. I would encourage you to think of something right now that you are grateful for. Now, imagine your life without it. I would venture to say it's hard to picture your life without it, right? Gratefulness keeps us grounded, knowing that we have everything we need for where we are right now. Appreciation encourages us to see the significance of the love we have not only in Christ but the ones around us too.

Somebody, Please Step In!

• Nearly 424,000 children are in foster care in the United States.

• On average, children remain in foster care for one and a half years; five percent of children stay in foster care for five years or longer.

• More than 23,000 children will age out of foster care every year after reaching eighteen; twenty percent of those will become instantly homeless.

It was a typical day. My sister and I had just arrived home, but no one was there. We sat and waited on the porch for our mother as usual. However, this day was different. We waited for what seemed like hours. It was cold, and we were hungry. The neighbors peeked out their door and asked had our mother got there yet; we shook our heads no. It was getting dark, and the street lights went out.

Suddenly my aunt began walking toward us, saying, "Joyce Ellen Isn't here yet? I'm going to go find her; you all wait here."

Not even moments later, the block was filled with police cars with their bright lights coloring the street red and blue. My sister and I didn't know what was going on. A woman came up to us and told us to get into a white van. We were cold, so we didn't hesitate. I thought she was going to let us sit in there until our mother came home.

While the van's back doors were open, I could see my mother pull up with my baby sister in her arms. She stood at the passenger-side door, trying to figure out what was going on. I'm not sure if anyone said a word to her. I vividly remember seeing someone taking my baby sister away from her, placing my mother in handcuffs, and then putting her into the back seat of a police car. She yelled, "Please don't take my babies!"

We sat in a room for hours, being questioned about everything. We had no idea who these people were. We wondered where our mother was and when she was coming to get us. Time passed, and then we were in the van again, our destination unknown.

We finally arrived at a house located at 127 West Ring Street. I hesitantly walked up to the door as my older sister walked alongside me. Inside the house, we were introduced to a woman named Ms. Wilson. The social worker explained to us that we would be staying with her for a little while. She told us that Ms. Wilson was a foster parent, and she helps children with a place to stay until their parents can get them. The lady seemed nice, and she made us a plate to eat right away.

That day turned into about seven years. While living there, I would visit my mother on weekends. I enjoyed that because it was like having the best of both worlds. I would get to see my mother and still feel the security of going back to my safe place. For me, visiting my mom was an opportunity to be around my sisters, which I loved. Most of the time, Mama would leave to go to her Narcotic Anonymous meetings. Sometimes, she would take us with her, but we'd opt not to go most times. On Sundays, my mother didn't hesitate to take us to church, which I hated. All the girls were often cliqued up, and my sister and I didn't fit in. I did enjoy listening to the choir sing, but everything else was far from me.

I stayed with Ms. Wilson, even when my sister left and went back to live with my mother. The social worker would check in periodically and ask if I was ready to go home. My answer was always no. I loved Ms. Wilson, and I knew she loved me. We would go to the women's center every Wednesday to talk to counselors and be around other foster children. I liked it; it gave me a sense of belonging.

I believe Ms. Wilson showed me the principles of love, and I will forever be grateful for that. It takes a special person to take care of someone else's children in a loving and motherly way. While living there, we had to do our chores, which consisted of washing dishes, folding laundry, cleaning our room, and keeping the basement (our play area) neat. I'll always remember how Ms. Wilson taught us to fold towels and miter the corners of a fitted sheet.

Ms. Wilson was a tough cookie when it involved following the rules. She didn't play, but we knew it was all in love. I will never forget the punishment that we received for being naughty. We would have to stand in the middle of the floor for hours without moving. Well, maybe it wasn't hours, but it sure felt like it. Ms. Wilson always expected the best from and for us. Even today, if she were alive, I know that I would be able to call or go over to her house and talk for hours.

For some, foster care isn't always so pretty. Don't get me wrong; we had our share of not-so-good days. However, my experience reveals to me that God's plan is a sure thing with an expected end, and all things are forever working for my good because I love him and I'm called according to His purpose.

Letters to God

FEELING VOID

Friday, 09/17/04, 10:34 p.m.

Dear Lord,

I don't know where to start. I know I haven't written to you, prayed, or even talked to you lately. I guess I thought I had it all together when I should have known I didn't. Lord, please help me. I feel terrible—sad, hurt, angry, and confused. I am confused because I don't know why I'm having all these different feelings.

I feel like I have nobody to talk to who will understand. I feel like I have to appear okay to everyone. Well, I'm not. Why don't I have any luck with my love life? I feel like I'm ready, but something assures me I'm not. Why is it when I need help from other people, no one can help me, but everybody always looks to me for help? I try hard to accommodate them.

I'm not happy. I know you love me, Lord, but I often feel alone. I don't have a close relationship with my mother, and unfortunately, I don't know my father. I often wonder, *Would my life be different with him in it?*

I have so many things happening to me simultaneously that I don't know how to react to anything. I feel blessed because you helped me get this job, but I'm still not happy. I felt good when you placed certain people in my life, but I'm still not satisfied.
I can see my attitude changing, and Lord, I need you to guide me in the right direction, because I think I'm going to fall. But I know you won't let me. Right now, I just pray that you stay by my side no matter what, because I know I let you down. I wish I had the answers, but we both know I don't.

Lord, I need you! Forgive me for my sins. Lord, lead me not into temptation but deliver me from all evil. Please don't forget about me, Lord. I love you always.

Wednesday, 11/11/2020, 11:49 p.m.

Dear Lord,

I pray that if anyone feels a void in their life because they have lost a loved one, you will comfort them. Please give them the peace that surpasses all understanding. My prayer is for girls who grew up without a father or had a strained relationship with their mother, that you would heal their hearts and restore their relationships. You are the Father who withholds no good thing. Thank you, Lord, that these things I've asked are already done in your precious Son Jesus's name. Amen.

Twenty-Twenty Vision

As I reflect, I chuckle at the idea of myself coming to the Lord with thoughts of self-pity. I was always having the question, *Why me?* I can imagine God looking at me and saying, *Why not?* I was battling with emotions that I didn't know how to direct. I now understand that I wanted the love every girl yearns for from a mother. I was lacking an identity of who I was from not knowing my father. I appeared lost in a sense, often searching for happiness outside of myself.

We all may sometimes find ourselves in a place of brokenness. The feelings of brokenness derive from a place of rejection. I often felt rejected when any relationship (friendship or romantic) failed. In hindsight, I believe this feeling was manifested from the disconnected relationship I had with my mother, father, and other family members.

This prayer gives me a sense of comfort in knowing that I was willing to depend on the Lord through it all. As human beings, we often find ourselves thinking about what we have and feeling like it's not good enough; we want more. Sometimes the question becomes Are we ready?

It is often in times of uncertainty that we can find ourselves building endurance and the resilience needed to walk out God's plan for our lives. If you find yourself in this place, I encourage you to seek happiness from within and let that be your guide to building overall satisfaction.

Somebody, Please Step In!

The Cycle Continues

- Three in ten American teen girls will get pregnant at least once before age twenty.
- Approximately 5.6 million abortions occur each year among adolescent girls aged fifteen to nineteen; about 3.9 million are unsafe.
- Parenthood is the leading reason teen girls drop out of school. More than fifty percent of teen girls never graduate from high school.

When I was about fourteen, I was trying to figure out who I was and where I belonged. I wondered who my father was and why my mother couldn't give me what I needed. During this time, I decided to move back with my mother. I was starting my freshman year of high school, and I remember wanting and needing emotional and physical support from my mom. Often it seemed that support was challenging for her to provide.

Being back in the home with my mother, I enjoyed the close relationship with my younger sisters, who were eleven, nine, and seven. My older sister and I often cared for them when my mother would be at one of her Narcotic Anonymous meetings or with whoever was her husband at the time. Things went on like this for some time. As a teenage girl, her absence was hurtful and left me feeling abandoned and rejected. I just wanted her to be there, spend time with her girls, take us shopping, have family outings, or cook for us sometimes.

When I was sixteen years old, I began having sex. I had no idea what I was getting myself into. Having sex wasn't a big deal to me until I found myself in a terrible predicament. I was feeling ill, sleeping in class, and not my usual self. My friends noticed the difference, and they suggested I might be pregnant. One day after school, two of my friends and I went to Cousins Subs, located on Twelfth Street in Milwaukee. My best friend had brought me a pregnancy test that we had planned for me to take. They both waited outside the bathroom stall as I took it. I sank onto the floor when I saw the bright pink lines and began sobbing.

My friends asked, "Mika, are you okay?"

I'm sure they felt my pain from the loud cries and knew that I wasn't. At that moment, we all knew my life was about to change. I was pregnant.

My friend hugged me and said, "Mika, it's going to be okay." I was devastated. I didn't know what to do, and I was afraid to tell my mother out of fear of what she would say or do.

Surprisingly, my mother was ecstatic. Her exact words were "I'm going to be a grandma" as she smiled with excitement.

I looked at her in disgust and said, "No, you are not." I didn't have a game plan of what I would do, but I was sure about one thing. I was not ready to be a mother. All my high school tasks, friends, and extracurricular activities started running through my head. I guess you can say I was a bit selfish, huh?

I told my mother I didn't want to have this baby, and she said, "Oh, no, you are not killing my grandchild."

I yelled at her in horror, "Are you going to take care of this baby?"

She responded with a yes. I knew that was not going to happen. From my perspective, she wasn't taking care of the kids she had. This experience was not the beginning of my broken relationship with my mother, but it was fuel to the fire.

I called my aunt and told her everything. She asked me what I wanted to do, and at thirteen weeks of pregnancy, I had an abortion.

My mother insisted she would not be a part of my plan or help me pay for it, so I rallied around people I could trust to help come up with the money. This experience left me feeling ashamed and negative toward myself. I couldn't understand if I made the right decision or not.

I carried this shame for a while; that is, until I became pregnant yet again at seventeen. This time I was accepting of it, happy even. I felt like I was in a relationship with someone that would last forever.

Well, little did I know, I would lose that child through a miscarriage because the baby was growing in my fallopian tube. The doctors said I could have died had I not got to the emergency room when I did. I spent three days in the hospital and almost missed my high school graduation. This experience left me feeling upset. *Why couldn't I have had that child?*

I began thinking God was punishing me for the decision I had made the year prior. Many years later, I started desiring to have a child again, but no matter how hard I tried, it didn't happen. I finally prayed to God, telling him that I felt so alone on the earth, and if he would bless me with a child, I would never have an abortion again. Still nothing.

This experience continued my cycle of feeling afraid, defeated, and depleted. Unsure of the unknown. I believe we all have these moments of uncertainty, but it's what we do in those moments that matter. The goal is to not stay there. Have a shift in your mindset. Become determined to acknowledge what you see, but don't let the circumstances define who you are meant to be. Often, we hear that you will make mistakes when you are young, but the truth is, most mistakes occur when we aren't taught anything different.

Letters to God

LAYING MY BURDENS DOWN: TRUST IN THE LORD
Sunday, 9/21/2003, 8:20pm

Dear Lord,

I want to walk closer to you, Lord. I know some of the things I do are not of your will, and that's the reason I'm writing this letter to you. Seeing how you know all things, you see and hear all things, I don't have to tell you some of the things I've done over the years, months, weeks, days, hours, and minutes. I just want forgiveness and to be able to walk down the path of righteousness.

For the past few months, things have been okay but not as good as they should be, and I know most of it is because I haven't been as faithful toward you as I should have. Now, Lord, on this day, I have decided to lay all my burdens down, trust in you, and prepare to receive all the many blessings you have in store for me. I pray that I will get back in school, fix my credit, get a new car, and have a healthy relationship with someone I love. I also pray that I begin to trust you more. All these things I ask in Jesus's name. Amen.

A PRAYER FOR YOU
Thursday, 11/12/2020, 12:29 a.m.

Dear Lord,

I pray for the women who feel a sense of discomfort in knowing if they have made the right decision about an issue concerning their heart. Lord, I pray that you would give them the wisdom they need to trust your plan for their lives. Help them to make decisions that will not only benefit them but increase the lives of others. If there is anything in their life that is not of you, I ask that you give them the strength to let it go. I pray for health and healing in their minds and bodies, in Jesus's name. Amen.

Twenty-Twenty Vision

As I reflect on my past prayer, I can see that I was a girl with goals. I believed that accomplishing my goals would help me push past the many shameful feelings of defeat that lay beneath the surface. I was overwhelmed with thoughts of failure and felt like receiving accolades and material things would ease my discomfort. Consumed with so many things I wanted to do, I had a knowing that I could only focus on what was in my control. At times, we focus on the things we don't have and fail to live thankful in the moment for the things we do have.

Looking back, I needed to create a focus. Choose one goal, make a step-by-step plan, and work toward achieving it. I believe creating so many deficits in our lives with our thinking can have us feeling depleted. One thing I can say I learned over the years is that Jesus is my righteousness, and he is the one I must stand before on judgment day. It was difficult then, always being fearful of making a mistake and concerned about what other people would say or think about me.

We have to come to a place where what we feel about ourselves is that we are good enough, in that we should always be thinking positive thoughts toward ourselves and making healthy decisions. Are we going to do everything right? I'm sure we won't; however, that doesn't mean we have to beat ourselves up about every circumstance that didn't work out so great. Show yourself some grace.

The Cycle Continues

Tragedy Strikes

- In the United States, drowning takes an average of 3,500 to 4,000 lives per year. That is an average of ten fatal drownings per day.
- Drowning is the number one cause of accidental death for children ages one to four.
- Drowning is the second leading cause of death up to age fourteen and fifth overall.

One day I took my fourteen-year-old sister to my boyfriend's house to visit him with me, which I had never done before. This day is significant because it was the last time I remember her saying something important to me. She said, "Mika, I want to be like you when I grow up." Initially, I thought, *No, you don't.* We began having a conversation regarding her statement, and I realized that I was looking at myself from my perspective instead of hers. What she saw in me, I didn't see in myself. She saw the good in me, or what I would like to call the God in me.

As individuals, we'll often focus on the wrong things about ourselves instead of the good. Why is that? I think sometimes it seems so much easier to do. I recall reading the book *Change the Way You See Everything* by Hank Wasiak and Kathryn D. Cramer. Even the words on the front cover of the book are written backward. In this book, the authors talk about having an asset-based way of thinking. This book is revolutionary and was incredibly life-changing and inspirational for me. It helps the reader to understand how to focus on your strengths, skills, talents, and virtues while not denying your weaknesses, faults, or shortcomings. It merely shifts your attention away from the negative energy they produce.

At the young age of seventeen, I had already adjusted to the idea that I had flaws, and I had allowed these flaws to become highlighted in my life (hence, not taking the positive remark from my sister and settling it into my heart).

I think of this moment often. It compels me to inspire others to want to be better, do better, and grow. If you're reading this book, I want to share with you how important you are, how relevant your life is to your family, children, spouse, or whomever your life has been destined to touch. You are enough, you are equipped to handle any situation that comes your way, and you are forever being perfected. You are a gift to those around you.

In April of 2000, I felt the joy of giving my full and entire life to Christ and the devastation of losing two sisters. I knew the moment that I gave my life over to Christ that I had a purpose, something bigger than myself to live for. What I didn't realize is that three months later, tragedy would strike. On July 28, three days after my eighteenth birthday, my two sisters, who were ten and fourteen, drowned and were washed away with the tide. It took emergency response teams and other personnel three days to find the youngest one.

I used to wonder if they felt any pain when they died. I researched what happens when someone is submerged underwater. What I found was astonishing. The water interferes with breathing due to the lack of oxygen. If you are in the water longer than four to six minutes without resuscitation, it causes death by suffocation. I thought it was ironic how water is so vital to life, yet it also had the power to take two of us.

Nothing of this magnitude had ever hit our family. One would think that this would bring us closer together, but the opposite occurred.

I remember the day it happened as if it were yesterday. I was on the bus headed home from work around 5:00 p.m. I was a dental assistant at Family Dental Center in Milwaukee, located on Thirty-fifth and Lisbon

Avenue. When the bus got near Thirty-fifth and Highland, I remembered that it was my friend's birthday. I reached up and pulled the yellow string to signify that I wanted to get off at the next stop. I hurried off, thinking, *Okay, I'm going to get her a birthday gift and drop it off quickly.* She didn't stay far from where the store was, and as I hurried toward her house, I reminded myself that I wouldn't stay long.

Not staying long turned into about 8:00 or 9:00 in the evening. Later, I got a call from my older sister, saying that I needed to get home because "Jensine needs some pads." I called my then-boyfriend and asked if he could drive me home. Of course, he made a big fuss about where I was and told me he wasn't taking me anywhere.

Annoyed, I hung up the phone and began walking. When I got about two blocks away from my house, my boyfriend's mother and father pulled up alongside me and told me to get in the car. They were hysterical, mentioning that something was wrong with my sisters. I quickly got into the car. I didn't know the conversation I'd had with my sister earlier was a ploy to get me home fast without causing me to panic.

As we arrived on the block, all I saw was red and blue lights on an unlit street. When I got out of the car, my aunt ran up to me, asking where my mother was. My heart was beating super-fast as I uttered, "I don't know."

She then said, "Jensine and Reba are gone."

It didn't register to me what she meant by gone. I responded, "Gone where?"

"We think they drowned," my younger sister interjected.

I instantly saw black, and when I woke up, I was in the back of a police car. I had fainted from the intense level of shock. While I was in the police car, the officers began asking me questions about my sisters' whereabouts. I yelled, "You all need to find them."

Later, rescue teams confirmed that they had drowned; they were gone.

The days leading up to the funeral seemed to all run together. I didn't want to sleep in the house, I couldn't eat, and I blamed myself. If only I had come straight home from work, they would still be here, I thought.

After the funeral, my mindset shifted. I began thinking, Why wasn't my mother there? Why did she take the phone from the house?

- Why did she not let them go with our grandma for the summer?
- Why did she get married again?
- Why don't they have a headstone?
- Why is she grieving the way she is?
- Why? Why? Why?

Questions continued to fill my head as I watched my mother lie in bed listening to Yolanda Adams song "Open My Heart" over and over and over again.

I grew tired of hearing that song, but it comforted me to an extent. Even now, when I listen to it, it always takes me back to that moment. I believe it was at that moment, seeing my mother lie there in despair, that the feelings of not being closer to her got worse. It seemed my mother was broken, lost, and confused, and I felt hopeless.

When I couldn't resolve the situation, I decided to continue my plans to attend college at UW–Parkside and reside on campus. My mother drove with me there and helped me unpack. She was so proud of me, but I could sense that she felt like she was losing me too. For some reason, I couldn't talk to her about what I was feeling. It was too hard.

I know that it was only through my firm foundation of faith and other women and friends' support that I healed past this experience. I believe God placed people in my path who could help me through this. I think we all need someone to walk with us through tough times of intense grief, pain, hurt, and loss. God has a way of sending the right person at the right time.

It seems life goes on when tragedy hits, and the expectation is for us to move right along with it. If you have suffered a loss recently, I will encourage you not to let the idea that we must get over it consume you. Give yourself permission to grieve and take as much time as you need. It may be essential to seek professional guidance as well.

Letters to God

LOVING YOURSELF PAST INSECURITIES

Saturday, 10/23/2004, 8:38 p.m.

Dear Lord,

I first want to thank you for continuing to bless me, although I'm not always deserving of it. Tonight, I want to talk to you about something very personal to me, and I need your help. Ever since my sisters passed away, I never really had an appetite, and Lord, now I believe it's getting worse. I don't know why sometimes I feel like eating, but I just don't eat. It's bizarre because sometimes I won't have a desire to eat at all. Then I will complain about being skinny.

Right now, Lord, I'm just asking you to provide me with the mindset to eat three meals a day (breakfast, lunch, and dinner). Lord, please give me the courage and faith to deal with the struggles I have in my life and the strength to cope with them. Help me to know that I am not alone. Lord, I'm asking you to give me an appetite and the means to fulfill it. I hope I don't have an eating disorder, but I'm starting to believe I do. It's like I don't like eating when I'm alone, and most of the time, I am by myself.
Lord, please don't let this new job stress me out to the point where I forget the purpose you set for me. Although I don't know what it is, I know you have one for me. Lord, I love you and always will. Just give me the strength to love myself enough to make the right decisions and do what's best for me.

A PRAYER FOR YOU

Thursday, 11/12/2020, 1:16 a.m.

Dear Lord,

Your Word says that you will heal the brokenhearted. I ask that your healing power will have its way in the life of the reader. I pray that if there is any sickness or disease, you would provide resolve. I pray that you will allow divine connections to take place to restore their bodies to health. Lord, because you know all, I pray that if someone struggles with an illness and is unsure what it is, you reveal it now.

Twenty-Twenty Vision

The prayer dated 10/23/2004 reflects some things about myself that I still struggle with at times. I believe that I had lost a sense of control in a particular area of my life. This sense of loss was creating symptoms in other unexpected places, like my eating habits. I figured since I could control what I put into my body, I consciously chose not to eat. The idea of looking in the mirror and continuously not liking what I saw was my vice. I used this as a coping mechanism to overcome grief, adopting the mindset of having a lack of control over something as simple as eating. We all know that we have to eat to live. In essence, I would say that at times I didn't feel like living. The lack of control over things that were happening in my life led me to disregard my health.

The last statement written in the past prayer still speaks volumes to me: "Just give me the strength to love myself enough to make good decisions and do what's best for me." When we have genuinely and wholeheartedly accepted ourselves, flaws and all, owning our insecurities and moving past disappointments and setbacks, we can embrace loving ourselves. Going through the grieving process of loss (end of a close relationship, a death, divorce, terminal illness) can leave you feeling anxiety or depression or even give you post-traumatic stress syndrome (PTSD).

The best way to move past negative emotions is to feel what you are feeling without judging yourself about it. Don't fixate on why something has happened or transpired the way it has. Instead, seek trustworthy people to talk to, try not to disconnect and withdraw, and remind yourself that what you feel is not permanent. Also, understand that you may go through all the grief process stages repeatedly and not always in order.

STAGES OF GRIEF

- denial and isolation
- anger
- bargaining
- depression
- acceptance

A wise person once said, "The best thing about feelings is that they come and go. Figure out what it is that remains after."

Enough Is Enough

- One in three women has experienced physical abuse by an intimate partner in their lifetime.
- Globally as many as thirty-eight percent of murders of women are committed by an intimate male partner.
- Violence can negatively affect women's physical, mental, sexual, and reproductive health.

College was a breeze; that is until I dropped out. I was getting good grades, making new friends, and having fun. But after a while, things got rough. I began having relationship issues, financial issues, and indecisiveness about a career.

I went back to Milwaukee, worked in a dental office full time, got my first small low-income-housing apartment on Twentieth and Galena, and attempted to live free from debt. I could never seem to get out of the hole. I prayed for some resolve, which resulted in me getting another job as a nursing assistant. Working two jobs helped a bit, but not much.

In the meantime, I was failing miserably at happiness in the romance department. The guy I was dating made me constantly feel worthless, hopeless, and insecure. At around age twenty-two, I remember focusing on the fact that all my friends were in relationships, settling down, and having kids. In contrast, I was feeling like life was passing me up. I continually thought I was in the world and in the way.

I repeatedly dealt with an ex-boyfriend I couldn't let go of emotionally, which kept me feeling sick and stuck. I would allow thoughts of what our relationship could become saturate my mind without looking at it for what it was—over!

I would continue accepting calls, going on random dates, having nightcaps, and allowing him to spew negativity into my life. Whether it be with his words or his actions, it was all too much. Two instances stood out in my mind that finally gave me the courage to walk away. I kept rehearsing them in my mind until one day it clicked, He doesn't want you, Tamika.

In the first instance, I found out that he had slept with my friend. I found myself walking down the street in a fit of anger, trying to fight this girl. My vision was blurred, not focusing on the fact that I shouldn't want to be with him. Rage had its way.

When she and I finished attempting to attack one another, I asked him, "Who do you want to be with?"

He looked at her, put up the peace sign, and replied, "It's been fun."

I smirked at that moment, feeling a sense of victory. As he and I began walking into the house, heading up the stairs, I had questions: why this, and how that; what reason did you do this and that? He turned around, looked in my face, and forcefully punched me. I gasped for air as I tried to catch my footing on the stairs. I couldn't believe it, but most of all, I couldn't believe I continued to walk up those stairs and stayed.

I sat on the bed and acted as if nothing had happened. At that moment, as I sat in that room, all I heard was the silence of shame. This incident wasn't the first time he'd let his anger get the best of him, but this was the moment I realized he didn't want me.

So, why did I stay? It's simple; all I wanted to do was strive to make him love me because the truth was, I needed that from him. If only I had tapped into what receiving love looked like sooner. This destructive on-and-off-again relationship wouldn't have continued for years and years.

The second instance persuaded me to examine the relationship and eventually leave. We were in the backyard, and I admit I was being spiteful, knowing that I was still sleeping with my ex-boyfriend although he was in a sexual relationship with someone else. And she was there too. The thought of him pretending nothing was happening between us upset me. I got jealous. I blurted out, "You were just at my house last night, though."

This remark sent him into a rage. He lunged toward me, clasped his hands around my neck, slammed me down into a pool of water, and held me there for a few seconds before others came and grabbed him.

This time I felt as though I was drowning. When I saw black, I knew that enough was enough; the moment I came up from the water, I knew I had to let go. I gasped for air and without thinking, I hauled off and started swinging. We were fighting like cats and dogs.

When it was all over, I had emotionally checked out.

I said enough was enough, but my actions said something else. I stuck around physically, although I knew that no amount of love was worth drowning for. One would think that would be it, but nope, I was stuck being stuck. I believed things would change if only I loved him a little deeper.

Feeling this way revealed my feelings of shame. Shame because I kept going back, shame because I didn't believe I deserved better, shame because I was afraid to leave, and shame because in my mind, I had lost. I felt defeated, thinking, *What does she have over me? Why did he pick her?*

Over time I realized that I first had to choose myself before anyone else could or would. It dawned on me that this had nothing to do with him or her, but everything to do with me. I began to look at myself as second fiddle, continually feeling used and abused. When I reached a depressive state, I knew things had to change.

This experience reminds me of a song a friend shared with me on *The Miseducation of Lauryn Hill*. In the song, she talks about how difficult it can be trying to be what someone else thinks of you. The lyrics say, "I made up my mind to define my own destiny." I realized that love could wait, or I could wait for the right kind of love.

43

I decided to shift my focus and went back to school, hoping for new opportunities.

Letters to God

JUST STOP
Friday, 9/26/2003, 12:38 a.m.

Oh Lord,

Today, I feel a change in me. I have always prayed and wondered what it felt like to have the Spirit move inside of me. Today you allowed me to see that, and I was ready. Now, Lord, I realize that I'm not perfect, but I'm going to try my hardest to walk in your Spirit. Today I have surrendered myself to you like no other.

You have placed some things on my heart that I must stop letting interfere with my relationship with you and the things you have in store for me. Here is a list of things I have decided to exclude from my life: First, stop having sex (my body is a temple, and I want you to use it as such). Second, stop cursing (for I know that the tongue is the wickedest part of the body, and I won't allow the devil to control my words). Third, stop letting the devil tempt me.

Thank you, Jesus, for allowing me to feel the change in myself. I know this is only the beginning. Satan will try to stop me, but I will always know that you're there waiting and watching over me. I love you, Lord. All these things I pray in Jesus's name. Amen.

WHEN SORRY IS JUST NOT GOOD ENOUGH
Tuesday, 03/23/2004, 9:54 p.m.

Dear Lord,

As I look back at the things I've written in the past few months, my heart feels heavy, and I just feel like crying. I know I have let you down once again, and I'm not even going to say I'm sorry. On second thought, yes, I am, because I am sorry. I know you're tired of hearing that, but you said to repent. I am so very disappointed in myself as I know you are too. I just don't understand how I know that the devil will attack yet still not be on guard to defeat him.

My life is not going the way I want it. Hopefully, it's going the way you plan. Today, or a little time before today, I realized that I don't like any of the guys I've been dating, and I'm getting sick of this. Why can't I stay with someone that I become so emotionally and physically involved with? I thought I knew what I wanted, but at this point, I have realized that I don't.

Lord, although I ask you for the same things repeatedly, please look past that and show me the way you want me to go. Please forgive me, Lord, and guide me in the right direction, for you know my heart.

PROMISES OF THE BROKEN

Sunday, 4/25/2004, 8:53 p.m.

Dear Lord,

I'm sorry it took me so long to write to you again. I've been feeling down lately, as you already know, but I think I'm back to my old self—well, I know I am. I have you to thank for that. It's funny how every time I say that I'm not going to let the devil defeat me, he finds a way to sneak back in, and he always seems to use my ultimate weakness. So now that I know the trick, hopefully I won't fall for it again.

When my ex asked me to go on a date, my mind said no, but my heart agreed. I guess my mind was playing tricks on me. As I listened to the pastor preach today about faith, it dawned on me that I was losing mine. But now I have found it, and I'm ready to walk again in your Spirit and go to the many heights you have in store for me. I have decided with your help that I will read my Bible every night, starting from the beginning until I get to the end. I want to know you better, Lord, and walk closer with you, and I realize that this is the only way to do it. Like my pastor says, "How can you have a friend and get to know them without learning and inquiring about them?" So, every night I'll say this prayer before I read: Lord, please help me to understand your Word and give me the strength to be obedient. Love always, your daughter. Thank you, Lord.

FEELINGS OF DEFEAT (FORGIVENESS)

Tuesday, 01/18/2005, 11:40pm

Dear Lord,

I have written how I let you down and how I need and want you to forgive me in my past writing. The truth that you possibly already know is that I am having a hard time forgiving myself, and that is why I have not yet turned away from the things in my life that are keeping me bound. I have let myself down extremely. I just don't understand how I was doing just fine and becoming a better person and woman; now, I just feel like I have no more hope. That is why I need you so badly, especially right now.

Lord, please give me the mind frame to forgive myself and give me the strength to let go of past things, people, and whatever else it is that you don't want to be a part of my life right now. On this day, I am making a change. I am ready to start over and endure all the good and bad things in store to become closer to you, Lord. I know it's not going to be easy because it never is, but I pray and surrender myself to you, and I know I will be okay.

I had sex at about 4:00 a.m., and I am making a promise to myself that this will be the last time until I can regain my focus, and you place me in the position where you want me. Hopefully, that's marriage or something along those lines. I need you, Lord because I cannot do this without you. Please don't allow me to be defeated, and I will surely try my best not to let you be either. Lord, please hear this prayer and realize the sincerity of it. I love you, and I want to make you proud.

Lord, give me the strength to step out on faith and obey your Word. Lord, if there is anything that you want me to know and do, please speak to me through your Spirit and show me the way. Lord, I am ready to fulfill your will for my life. Lord, give me the power to forgive myself as I know that everyone makes mistakes and gets weak at times. Tell me what you want me to hear, and give me the mind to understand what the Spirit is saying to me.

A PRAYER FOR YOU
Friday, 11/13/2020, 5:59 p.m.

Dear Lord,

Thank you for healing me of feelings of brokenness. I pray that if anyone reading this book feels broken right now, you will transform their hearts by the renewal of their minds. I pray that if any woman struggles in an abusive relationship, you will give her the strength to know her worth. I pray that she will have the courage to seek help for herself and her family. I pray that she will no longer hide her scars to protect an image others may have of her. In Jesus's name, I pray. Amen

Twenty-Twenty Vision

As I reflect on all the past prayers in this section, I notice that I wanted to see my life look different. I was tired of doing the same things and expecting different results. I wanted to trust God with my whole heart. In turn, I decided to give up my fleshly way of thinking for a Spirit -led mindset. The main thing I realize is that Satan is not the only tempter or adversary. It was often the inner me that inhibited me from walking closer with the Lord. I needed to consciously stop doing what I didn't want to do and create new habits to change my actions.

I can admit that I sought love in all the wrong places. I desired to serve and have a relationship with God but continued to find myself in situations where I craved a man's affection to feel loved and validated. I often turned to sex as an opportunity to shield myself from the lack of affirmation from a father and the insecurity of being alone. When I found myself being tempted by my fleshly desires, I needed to say no; however, sex had become the one moment where I felt like someone wanted me. I didn't realize that I deserved more. Now I understand that true repentance requires changed behavior.

I laugh at the repetitiveness of what I would call my ultimate weakness (sex with my ex). The idea of feeling not good enough kept me broken. I thought I would gain endless affection if I gave my body to another. However, I only seemed to fall deeper into my brokenness. Many people would not be able to tell this from my attitude and outward appearance. I felt disconnected from my family, which left me feeling alone.

Having the closeness of family is what I craved. I always found myself clinging to older women who seemed like a mother to me. I even found myself staying in relationships with people who weren't the best influence because I hated feeling rejected or void. Letting go had become the hardest thing for me to do in any relationship. I'm sure many of you can relate to this.

I was a woman who repeatedly let the desire for love bring feelings of shame and defeat. I could not stop doing the one thing that I said I did not want to do. In the Scriptures, Paul talks about doing something that he does not want to do (The Holy Bible, English Standard Version, 2001, Romans 7:15–20). I wonder about the thorn he speaks of in his flesh, which ultimately is some form of weakness. I notice that my thorn or weakness was the sin of fornication. I seemed sure that I wanted to be married. Looking back, I'd say I wanted to experience love from being in a committed relationship with intentions to appreciate sex without regret after.

Over time I had to learn to do and not just say. I've also realized that accountability is vital. The best way we can heal from our brokenness is to take a self-inventory. Identify areas of dis-ease and tackle them head-on. I had to consciously tell myself, "I am Tamika. I have the power to change my circumstance, and I deserve better not only from other people but from myself too." Creating boundaries was essential for me when growing past this experience. Boundaries help us become accountable and show others how we expect and want them to treat us. Remaining consistent will take an intentional level of discipline and determination.

Keep in mind that sex is not something God made with shame in mind. He created it with us in mind to join two people through body, mind, and spirit within marriage. It is intended to be an act of love. Knowing this, we need to understand that love is not a mere feeling but an intentional decision followed by action. Love is two people mutually agreeing to come together unselfishly by giving of themselves to one another.

If you're single and walking out this kingdom lifestyle that God has purposed for us, I'm sure you may have struggled with sexual temptation at some point or another. I have learned that we are not perfect beings. No matter how hard we try, we will sometimes fail. However, when we do, we must not let condemnation settle in our hearts, which causes us to grow further away from Christ.

God wants us to draw near to him whether we think we're doing everything right or not. Drawing near to him will help us create new habits as we learn more about who he is in our life. We must be steadfast in our mindset and stick with our decisions if we choose not to have sex for some time. In a practical sense, situations in which we may become tempted to sin are ones that we should avoid. I know how difficult this can be for some because I dealt with it firsthand. However, talking with your mate openly about your feelings toward having sex before marriage is a great starting point when you're in a healthy, committed relationship. When they see the relationship's direction, you both can be on the same page and hold one another accountable. If this is not possible for you, find a friend you trust to hold you accountable to your Word through prayer and encouragement.

Father, Can You Hear Me?

• More than one in four children live without a father in the home; they are forty-seven percent more likely to live in poverty.

• Children who live without a father in the home are at greater risk of behavioral problems, abuse, and neglect; seven times more likely to become teen parents; two times more likely to drop out of high school; and more likely to go to prison.

• Children with involved dads are less likely to be mistreated.

Father, can you hear me? I continuously asked that question in my early adult years. I felt so alone and needed someone to listen. I would often ask myself, *Would my life be different if my father were in it?* One early morning around 1:00, after I let my older sister stay at my place, we got into an argument. I recall the statement she made to me: "You're jealous of me because I know who my father is, and you don't."

I said the only thing that came to my mind at that moment. "I know who my father is; he is God in heaven, and he takes good care of me." I don't remember her response, but I felt liberated and dismayed simultaneously after saying that. Liberated because that was my truth, and I stood in it. Dismayed because knowing my father was a deep desire of my heart. The Bible says that the Lord will give you the desires of your heart. The only thing we must do is trust in the Lord and do good, delighting ourselves in the Lord (The Holy Bible, English Standard Version, 2001, Psalm 37). I believed this Scripture wholeheartedly.

About a year after that argument occurred, my mother called me one day and said, "Mika, I found your father."

She had always told me my father's name, and from childhood on up, I had created an image in my mind about how he looked and how he would act toward me if I ever met him. I remained calm about the situation, saying, "When can I talk to him?"

My mom continued in excitement, "They live in Illinois, and they want to meet you."

I suddenly became nervous. I couldn't believe this was really about to happen.

On my twenty-fourth birthday, I met my stepmother, brother, sister, uncles, aunts, grandmother, and most importantly, my father. They rolled out the red carpet for me. My uncle did my hair and makeup; my dad showered me with gifts, including a Chanel ring; and they threw me a huge birthday party. I felt like a princess. My dad kissed me on my forehead and said, "I love you, sweetheart, and I'm sorry I missed so much of your life."

Those words were like gold to me. I forgave quickly. I drove back to Milwaukee on cloud nine. When I arrived back home and told family and friends about my newfound family, some were happy for me, but some created doubt.

As I continued to talk to my father over the phone, I began to feel a pressing in my spirit to know for sure. I wanted to be able to silence the naysayers with concrete proof. I suggested to my father that we get a DNA test. He initially disagreed, his exact words being "I know you're my baby girl." Those words gave me so much security at that time.

Before we went forward with taking the test, I recall standing in his living room and him saying, "I hope this test doesn't come back wrong."

My response was "It's going to come back right, and it will be the truth."

For my entire life that I can remember, I have sought to know the truth. Over time I learned to brace myself for the results. The results were finally in—he was not my father.

After receiving those results, I was devastated. I went to my mother's house. She also lived in Illinois at the time. I told her the outcome, and her only response was "So all this time, Johnnie was your father."

I was disappointed with that being all she had to say. I stood there waiting for more like a deer caught in the headlights, but nothing. I felt sad, confused, and angry because, yet again, my mother was not there for me the way I needed her to be. By now, I was beginning to accept this realization as the norm between her and me. While driving home to Wisconsin, I told myself I wasn't talking to her anymore. Immediately I could feel a nudge in me saying, *Yes, you will, because that's your mother.*

Feeling broken, I started to think a mother's love could never exceed the love of a child or daughter. I felt like I had forgiven her time and time again, with my feelings left crushed. It was as if I had no father or mother.

As I continued to talk to God about this situation, I was comforted. I knew that part of my healing process would be to discontinue talking to the family I had recently met, loved, and thought was my own. Growing up, I always felt like I would embrace and become a part of other people's families instead of having a healthy relationship with my own. I didn't think I could take another attachment like that, especially one that created such turmoil for me on the inside. About six or seven years later, the man that I knew as my father from childhood died. When I found out about his death, it was as if I had lost him twice.

About four years after the shocking DNA results, my sister called me and said that she thought her father was mine. Her supporting evidence was that he had a daughter that looked just like me. By this time, I was so over finding out who my father was, but when she said he wanted to meet me, I obliged. When I first saw this man, I knew he was my father. I didn't know how I knew; I just knew. He was happy to meet me, but this meeting was nothing like the meeting with father number 1. The meeting with father number 1 was comfortable, safe, and loving. This meeting felt strained and distant. I can't put my finger on the difference.

I suppose it may have been because I had already felt disappointment with the first situation. I told my dad the story about what happened with father number 1. He then shared with me that he was at the hospital when I was born and said to my mother, "This isn't my baby, but I'm going to take care of her like she is." It seemed the right thing to do because he and my mother were married at the time. He then jokingly commented, "If you are not my baby, you will be my lady." My sister and I found these remarks disturbing and uncomfortable, but we laughed along. About a few weeks later, we took a DNA test. The results came back, and he was my father. We talked a bit after, and I visited him a few times.

A couple years went by before we saw each other again. When we did, the unthinkable happened. I will never forget this day and the extreme level of disappointment it brought. I was getting ready to head back to Milwaukee and was dropping him off at home. As I arrived close to the location where he wanted to get out, he asked for a kiss goodbye on the lips as he leaned toward my face. I told him I didn't feel comfortable with that, but he insisted, stating, "I kiss all my babies on the lips."

I responded and said, "Okay, well, I'm not a baby. I'm a grown lady."

He proceeded to say, "Yeah, but you're my baby."

As I sat there in the driver's seat looking at him with impatience because he had had too much to drink, I said, "You can kiss my cheek."

I leaned over. I then felt his tongue on my lips, attempting to enter my mouth. I was horrified. "Get out!" I shouted as I reached over and opened the passenger door for him.

He yelled, "I'm sorry," as I pushed him by the shoulder out of the car door. I sped away, feeling confused. Why had this happened to me? It reminded me of a time just weeks prior that a male coworker had done a similar thing.

I felt terrible wondering, *What should I do? What should I say? Do I tell people?* I was humiliated; I never wanted to utter a word of this situation to anyone. Then it hit me. *Tamika, you can't be silent about this. Your dad or not, this is not your shame to carry.*

The first person I called and told was my husband. He couldn't even believe it. For years I wondered, *Why do these types of things keep happening to me? Is there some sort of signal that I am giving off that makes men feel like they have the right to assault me sexually?* My trust issues intensified after this experience. I began thinking men were dishonest, and I started to question everything anyone said to me, always believing that I'm bound to find a lie. A mindset such as this is a difficult way to live.

Reflecting on these two experiences in my life, I can identify with my younger self realizing that coming into my own was a necessity. I was not moved by what others thought or had to say. I learned to mask my feelings entirely. I often talked to God about my desires and acknowledged him openly. I sought to know who I was and where I came from. In essence, I remember when God began to move in my life. Because God is not the author of confusion and his Word says that the truth shall set you free, as situations arose, they brought forth the manifestation of the desire of my heart. I would go further to say more than likely the hearts of others too.

I've come to understand that things don't always turn out as we plan. Although the decisions we make in our lives today may have a lasting effect on other people's lives in years to come, that doesn't mean we don't acknowledge our mistakes. Nothing can remain hidden forever. The truth will always come to light. I challenge you to accept the decisions you've made in the past and identify if your actions may have hurt someone in your life. If so, apologize, empathize, and open your heart to new beginnings. I encourage you who have been on the receiving side of the hurt to forgive and open your heart to new beginnings, whether it includes the person who hurt you or not. Remember, forgiveness is not a feeling; it's a decision.

Letters to God

REVEAL YOUR WILL

Wednesday, 09/08/06, 7:45 a.m.

Dear Lord,

First of all, I would like to say thank you. You have been so good to me. I love you. I have been thinking about writing to you for some time. I just haven't sat down and done it. I guess I feel like it's time.

Lord, over the past year, you have shown me the things that you want me to do. Every time you do new things in my life, it always amazes me, not because I don't believe it, but because I'm forced to acknowledge that it was you.

Today is when we (my dad and I) get our DNA test results. Something assures me that he is my father, but I still feel nervous about the whole thing. Lord, whatever happens, please prepare me for it and give me the strength and wisdom to accept and understand the outcome. I pray for strength, wisdom, courage, and patience. I am waiting, watching, and listening.

Lord, I ask that you anoint me with the Holy Spirit to do your will for my life. Bless my family, friends, loved ones, and the whole world. Please send me the answers to my questions that I don't know. I don't remember them all, but you do. Thank you for working in my life, and please continue to work through me for your name's sake. I love you and always will. Amen

A PRAYER FOR YOU

Sunday, 11/15/2020, 1:36 p.m.

Dear Lord,

I pray for every little girl and young woman who seeks to know who her biological father is. I pray that you would give them the desires of their hearts. I pray that if there are any feelings of hurt, unforgiveness, or discouragement from them not knowing their father, you will comfort them. I pray that you give them the answers they seek and connect them with the people who can help them. I pray that they will not lose hope but recognize that with God, all things are possible. In Jesus's name, I pray. Amen.

Twenty-Twenty Vision

Reflecting on the past prayer, I was a woman who was excited about knowing my birth father but also showing signs of doubt. I asked God to settle any feeling of uneasiness in my heart and to give me understanding before I even received the truth.

When we can sense the truth in our spirit, it is important to be obedient to that unction. When we are disobedient to what the Lord tells us, we will surely pay the cost. We see people falling away from Christ because they see shame in their lives and believe everyone else can see it too. It's important to understand that spiritual death is a real thing. Spiritual death is merely separation from God. Our sins make us unclean, and we feel like we are unable to dwell in the presence of God. We need to understand that sin is merely missing the mark from what God has purposed and planned for us. The good news is that Jesus Christ offers redemption from this when we choose to have faith in him, repent of our sins, and obey the principles of the gospel.

Wait for Love

• Sixty percent of couples who marry between the ages of twenty and twenty-five will end in divorce, while those who marry after twenty-five are twenty-four percent less likely to divorce.

• Fifteen percent of adult women in the United States are divorced or separated today.

• Seventy-three percent of marriages end because of lack of commitment, fifty-five percent because of infidelity, and forty-one percent because of lack of preparation.

Waiting for love seemed like torture, but I knew it was time to move on from what felt like dysfunction. I was content with focusing on work and being alone. I had become accepting of the notion that I would have to wait an indefinite amount of time for Mr. Right.

I had just left work from being forced to work overtime, and I still had on my corrections uniform. I hoped I didn't see anyone I knew because I didn't feel like talking, but the uniform usually deterred people from making conversation. As I stood in the Family Dollar Store, struggling to figure out which bottle of oil I should buy to settle my engine from overheating, I hear a deep voice say, "You need some help picking out that oil?"

"No," I replied in a way that meant *Please don't say anything else to me.*

He smirked and said, "I don't mind putting the oil in your car for you if you need help."

"All right. Thank you," I replied.

When he looked at my car, it seemed to need more work than I expected, a new engine. I wasn't financially prepared to handle this type of repair. I panicked, thinking about having to be at work that night without any imaginable way of getting there. He must have sensed my frustration because he offered to take me home and fix my car since he was a mechanic. Later I found how he wasn't a mechanic at all. When I couldn't get the car fixed, he offered to take me to work and pick me up. This went on for several months.

He continued to ask me out on dates and make other friendly gestures to show he liked me. I told him that he wasn't the type of man I was interested in dating, but he was persistent. As time went on, I decided to give him an opportunity thinking, *Maybe this "different" type of man is what I need.* I began to inquire about his life, family, and personal information.

He was not real forthcoming with information, and sometimes his explanations didn't make sense to me, but I overlooked it. As we continued to talk, I shared with him my insecurities and my thoughts on being in failing relationships and wanting to settle down. He assured me he was different.

As time went on, I became pregnant. I couldn't believe it. After all the years of wishing and hoping to have a baby, it had finally happened. I was called to motherhood. Although I felt I didn't deserve it, I was happy. Not having a strong relationship with my mother left me feeling like I would become a distant mother like I thought she was. I struggled for years, trying not to be like my mother until it dawned on me that I couldn't become like her in the way I imagined because I wasn't her.

I was ecstatic at the thought of being able to raise my first child. When I told him I was pregnant, he seemed happy too. Then everything came tumbling down once I found out things that I would never have imagined about this man, something that made me cringe, want to walk away, and be in absolute fear. There rose those underlying feelings of shame and defeat again. I wondered why he didn't tell me these things. The answer was evident. He knew I would walk away or at least had a strong inkling that it was a possibility.

The thought of not having the baby crossed my mind, but my inner spirit would not let me go down that road again. This time it was different, and I wasn't only thinking about myself. I loved the baby that was growing inside of me. The notion that I would have a human being in my life that I could finally love and who would unconditionally love me impressed upon my being. This baby was what I needed to feel a sense of growth and the possibility of moving on.

I pushed past my feelings of fear and doubt, which some would call red flags in this relationship, and I decided to stay for the baby. I convinced myself that I could grow to love this man and set aside all the hurt and confusion. Three years later, we were divorced.

Later I began dating the man I cheated on my ex-husband with. This relationship felt different, unforced even. I seemed to have a friend in this man. I felt like he understood me, wanted the best for me, and loved me. Before we first started dating, he would jokingly say I love you every time he saw me. He didn't even know me, so I would laugh because I knew he couldn't have seriously meant that. We would talk on the phone for hours about almost anything.

Then things shifted. I was beginning to want more of a commitment from the relationship. I think me wanting more made him resistant to establishing if this relationship is what he wanted. I shared with him my faith, and he wasn't digging that. He accepted my beliefs but made it clear he wasn't on the same page. I was okay with that because my prior experience had left me not wanting to deal with any man that claimed to be of the Christian faith. I made sure it was clear to him that I didn't want to get married considering the previous outcome of a decision such as that. He was cool with that too.

As our relationship progressed, we started spending more time together. He was around my son more, and he introduced me to his children as well. Eventually, we decided to move in together. Living together was okay, but it was something that I had said I would never do unless I were married. Ultimately, I had lived up to this conviction, at least until this point. Never say never, right? For me, I felt like it was okay to do things differently than I had done before simply because I expected different results.

My then-boyfriend and I lived together and were in a committed relationship for about two years before we married. I believe I lived under a certain level of grace for a while because I didn't feel convicted about dating, living, and sleeping with him without being married. That grace lifted after some time. I began feeling uncomfortable internally each time I would have sex with him. I tried not to let it bother me, but it did. I talked with him about it, but he didn't understand the level of my conviction.

One day after attending a church service, I had a conversation with a friend about how I was feeling. As we talked, she said, "Well, I don't know how you can expect this relationship to work, considering how it started." I was shocked to hear that come from her mouth, but I dismissed it. Later that week, I went to church to attend a praise team rehearsal, and my pastor advised me that I would have to sit out. I questioned his reasoning behind this, and his response was because I was living with my boyfriend. I was sad because I had a desire to worship in song. I talked to my boyfriend about this, and he thought it was ridiculous. I tried to rationalize the decision with him, but he felt like it wasn't right.

One day while driving to a friend's house, I began saying a prayer in my mind to God. I asked him if I should continue to be with Robert because I didn't feel like I could trust him fully. When I finished praying, my prayer was answered by my four-year-old son sitting in the back seat. He said, "Mama, my dad was your husband; Robert is going to be your ex-husband."

I was flabbergasted. I couldn't believe he had just said something like that. I turned around to face the back seat, looked at him, and said, "What did you say?"

He repeated, "I mean, my dad is your ex-husband. Robert will be your next husband."

Being that he was four, I questioned the way he said what he said. I went back in prayer and said, "Okay, Lord, now I'm confused." Imagine that. We get our answer, and then we question it because it didn't present itself the way we expected.

When I arrived at my friend's house, I told her what had happened. We then noticed that my son was telling all the other kids how his "dad" has the same game at home that they were playing. In my spirit, that was God confirming that what my child had said to me was not to be dismissed.

Later, I went home and told Robert what he had said. He laughed and said, "Well, at least I'm gone be your husband."

We chuckled together. Then I said, "No, because divorce is not an option if we get married." At that moment, we had solidified our decision on what it meant for us to get married and stay married.

A few weeks went by, and after thinking about what I was going to do, I went to my pastor and told him that I wanted to marry Robert but wasn't sure if it was time yet. I expressed to him that I asked Robert if we could live apart until we got married. My pastor then offered a place that he owned for Robert to stay.

Later that day, I shared the information with Robert, and he disagreed with that idea. I then asked him if he would be okay with not having sex and still living together. His response was "If that's what you want to do." We tried this for a little bit and finally decided to get married.

Our wedding was quite simple, with it being at the church with two witnesses (my aunt Ifama and one of his friends). It was sweet how he proposed to me the day before our planned wedding while lying in bed. He lay at the foot of the bed, and pulled a heart-shaped ring out of his pocket, and said, "Will you marry me?"

I smiled and replied, "I already plan to tomorrow." We both laughed, and my husband and I have been married for seven years now.

I share this story to say that even if we make an unfavorable decision that changes our life's direction, it doesn't equate to us having to live the rest of our lives thinking we are unworthy of love or marriage. By committing that one indiscretion in my first marriage, I felt like I didn't deserve to be in this committed one. I often had expectations and suspicions that my husband would cheat on me. This overwhelming feeling of mistrust came from my inner feelings of unworthiness. The truth is, we cannot keep holding ourselves in bondage, self-sabotaging the good that is in front of us because of our past faults. Forgive yourself, repent, and move on.

Letters to God

REPENTANCE

Thursday, 03/03/11, 12:09 p.m.

Dear Lord,

I know it has been a long time since I sat down and wrote to you. I usually just talk to you daily, but I guess the things that are important to me I write it out to see the growth and change that happens to take place over time. Lord, I love you, and I know you know that. I feel like I have made the biggest mistake of my life by getting married. Sometimes I wonder, Why did you let me do that? Why didn't you stop me?

Then I can hear your voice telling me, I tried to.

Lord, as I sit here in tears, I just am ultimately sorry. Again, I feel like I stepped outside of your will for my life. Lord, please bring me back. Lord, forgive me for cheating on my husband. I just don't understand why I did that.

I know how sacred marriage is. As you know, I moved out on my own with my baby in November. I know you were the one who directed me to do so, but sometimes I feel scared and wonder, Should I just try to work my marriage out? But how? Now that I believe I know what love is, it's hard for me to force it with him. I love him as the father of my child, but my heart is not with him at all. I feel like I have messed everything up, and I'm just leaning on you to fix it. I don't know what the future holds, and that's what honestly scares me. Although I am deep in sin, Lord, please forgive me and help me to do your will for my life.

Sunday, 11/15/2020,4:17 p.m.

Dear Lord,

If anyone is reading this and struggles with any type of sin in their life, I hope you will strengthen them in your Word. I pray that you would remind them that there is no condemnation for those in Christ Jesus. I pray that they would come to an understanding that you want them to walk closer to you. I pray for your wisdom and peace that surpasses understanding will manifest in their lives right now. In the name of Jesus, I pray. Amen

Twenty-Twenty Vision

As I reflect on this prayer, I realize that nothing can replace the work I needed to do on myself. I couldn't expect to get married and think it would solve the inner feelings of loss, insecurity, and defeat. I got married for all the wrong reasons feeling as though I could right a wrong, then consult God to fix it afterward. Entering into a marriage to prove to others that I could move on from my past was a huge mistake that left me feeling stuck and unloved. I had inadvertently masked my imperfections behind someone else's flaws. Although I desired to make things work for my son, ultimately, I knew that wouldn't appease my inner being. I was unconsciously self-sabotaging because I wanted to do what most would consider the unthinkable. The guilt wouldn't let me keep my unfaithfulness a secret. Although he tried to stay with me, I couldn't see that being possible.

I am encouraged by the idea that I had the heart to forgive. I was a woman who did not fully understand that Jesus is my righteousness. In hindsight, I know I'm nowhere near perfect. We all have flaws or things in our lives that make us less than perfect, yet God still sees perfection and is continuously perfecting us. There is no shame in life's past. Guilt comes when we wear the mask acting as if we're okay. I would encourage you not to ignore any red flags, seek God for wisdom, and don't be afraid to change your mind, especially if you're getting ready to walk down the aisle. Regardless of what the outcome may be or what other people may say, make a decision that you're willing to live with.

We can never adequately right a wrong. We must consider that what's done is done, and we must live and learn from our mistakes. It's important to accept and acknowledge our truth even if the other person refuses to. When dealing with other people, we should always give them the gift of choice. Don't let someone believe that something is what it is not. Be honest in all your dealings. If you want to be in a relationship with someone and you think they will not choose you because of something in your past, don't hide it; reveal it and let them decide. Even if the result is not what you had hoped for, trust that God will work things out on your behalf. If one door of opportunity closes, remember there is always another, and this time, it will have your name on it.

Redefined Life

I hope you have gained insight from this book, understanding that there will always be an opposing force that will try to work against your life's calling or destiny. I call these circumstances, situations, and decisions that we make. Circumstances and conditions are sometimes not in our control. However, many choices that we make are. My question to you is, What is driving the decisions that you are making? Is it your circumstance or situation? Is it your emotions and feelings, or is it that small inner voice of the Holy Spirit?

There are times when we have to make quick decisions in life, and then there are other times when we can settle in and listen to the small still voice for guidance. My prayer for you is that you tap into your inner man to fulfill your destiny. Here is one way that you can do that. I bet you can already guess what I'm about to say. Yes, you got it, prayer. The Word says to pray without ceasing and in all things give thanks. Our hearts should remain bent toward prayer. We will then start to notice things aligning in our lives and manifesting what we speak.

If you don't believe me, let me share a testimony with you. I can remember praying with my pastor for maybe a year before I could even see how God would move in my life to answer the desired prayer. As we prayed, I heard the Lord say, "Now it's your job just to believe," and I did just that.

I had been praying to have a child with my husband. It took me a long time to get to the place of even accepting that that was my heart's desire. When I met my husband, he had a vasectomy, so I had already contended with the idea that we would not have children. For one, he didn't want any more children, and besides, it was physically impossible.

When the desire became stronger and stronger, I knew that this wasn't just something that I wanted, but I believe it was destined to manifest in our life. I went to my husband and began talking to him about it. For a long time, he was steadfast in the fact that his answer was no.

Later something happened; God softened his heart in this area, and one day when we talked about it, his response was shockingly different. He said, "Yes, I'll get a reversal, but I'm not paying for it."

I said, "Okay." I took that yes and ran with it, not knowing where the funds would come from. I trusted God to bless us and give me the desire of my heart. I started making doctor appointments, making sure my body was healthy enough and prepared to have a child. When meeting with specialists, they explained all our options. Initially, we were thinking of doing in vitro fertilization (IVF); however, after further consideration, we realized that was the least cost-effective with no definite positive results. We finally decided to go with the reversal plan, which was $7,000. I remember crying, praying to God, saying," I have no idea where this money will come from."

But God! I continued walking it out as if things were already paid for and figured out. I let go and stopped worrying about how the story would play out.

We scheduled the appointment, and my husband and I later found out that my mother's husband won the jackpot. The Holy Spirit told me to ask him for the money. I was scared, reluctant, and almost refused to ask. I decided to be obedient and asked him. Through this experience, I finally understood the gift of the "ask." I will never forget his response. He looked at me and said, "How much do you need?" I told him the amount. He then said, "Whew, Mika, that's a lot of money." He proceeded to say that he wouldn't be able to give us the full amount, but he would lend us some of it.

I was so grateful I told him that anything would help, and I just appreciated his heart toward this situation. He then looked over at my mother and said, "You think I should give her the full amount?" My mom looked at him and shook her head yes. He then counted out $7,000 in cash and put it into my hand.

My mom and I stood in the kitchen and hugged with tears in our eyes. She said, "Mika, I'm so happy we could do this for you all." I will never forget that moment. My faith has always been strong, but at that moment, I knew without a shadow of a doubt that God is a miracle worker. He causes things to align in ways we can't even imagine if we just put our trust in him.

The enemy wasn't too far behind, waiting to steal our blessing. About a month later, my car was totaled while parked in front of my job. In addition to that, I was in bankruptcy. They were telling me that my car replacement didn't qualify under the bankruptcy terms, meaning I would have to be without a vehicle.

I continued to pray, knowing that this situation had already been figured out. I battled with the idea of using the money that was put up for the surgery to get a car, but my heart wouldn't let me do it. I trusted that God would provide for me. When we finally went to have the procedure, we learned there was a seventy percent chance that we would have a child, and it might take up to about a year before my husband's "fish would be swimming again."

My husband's surgery was on July 27, 2017, and I was pregnant by the end of August 2017. We had a beautiful, healthy baby boy full of life on May 3, 2018.

That's not all of this story of God's amazing grace. A few weeks after I found out I was pregnant, the credit company called me and said, "We've come to a resolve. We're going to allow your new vehicle to replace the totaled one, and you can go pick it up from the dealership today." So I had a car to bring my baby home in.

Nothing is too hard for God. Period!

I will suggest that you remember when praying out God's will for your life that if it includes other people, you must consider their will as well. In the above instance, it was important for my husband to agree with my desire for it to manifest itself in the natural.

We should continuously be praying for the nations and trusting God to do what he has promised. When we get and remain in the position of our calling, we will see change, not only change in our lives but a difference in the world around us. Prayer connects us to the Father like a lifeline. The critical thing is that you must believe with your whole heart without wavering. Talk to God, listen, love, and forgive. Understand that challenges in life push us to become our better selves. After all, no one is perfect, but we can all strive toward being better.

Letter to God

GOD'S WILL FOR YOUR LIFE
Monday, 01/03/05, 11:25pm

Dear Lord,

As you can see, it's a whole new year. I want to thank you for watching over me and providing for me for the past year and pray that you'd continue to do so this year. Lord, you have brought me a long way and allowed me to see and experience many things, and it was all for your glory. Thank you, Lord, for revealing yourself to me this year, and I pray that you continue to work in my life and just instill in me the patience that I need to fulfill your will.

Lord, if I have let you down in anything that I have done, I apologize right now. Lord, I know you know my heart, and I just wish you would allow the desires of it to be done. I want you to help me start this new year off right, and I'm going to try my hardest not to let you down, but Lord, I'm only human. I know you know what's been going on in my life, and I just can only hope and pray that you would reveal your will to me for my life. What do you want me to do? Why are certain people still in my life? Why can't I move on? Is it because I'm not willing to let go, or is it more significant than that? I have still been feeling lonely.

Lord, I know that mostly when I write to you, I'm asking for things for me, but tonight I want to pray for your people. I know you're looking over them, and many of them are in the testing phase that they must overcome. Lord, I ask that you give them the strength and knowledge they need to endure. Please reveal yourself to them and bless them with all the things they need. Lord, I also pray for my family and friends. Amen

Twenty-Twenty Vision

As I reflect on this prayer, I see myself as a woman who still hasn't tapped into the fullness of who God is in my life. I constantly question myself and the decisions I make. I felt helpless when depending on the humanistic side of myself. The prayer sounds like one of a longing heart, but one that doesn't understand what it's longing. I felt stuck, stuck in my past, hoping to walk into a future that I could not see. I challenged myself to open my heart toward the needs of others who may need God's strength to overcome.

When we choose to stop living according to our flesh and walk by the Spirit, life circumstances will affect us differently, in the most humbling way that we can imagine. We will become less focused on self but more so on how we show up for and in other people's lives. We all have a divine awakening, something that propels us to not only want better but to do better too. The Word says that I can do nothing in and of myself, but through Christ, who strengthens me, I can do all things (King James Version, Philippians 4:13). Letting go can seem hard at times but understand that it's time if you sense that beckoning in your spirit.

Understand that being alone is the physical state of not being around another person, whereas loneliness is a mindset. It's characterized by a distressing experience when your relationships are self-perceived to be less in quality and quantity. You might be alone during times of freeing yourself, but you don't have to feel lonely. When you love yourself and don't have unrealistic expectations of others, this shields you from the attitude that loneliness causes. I believe that many times we expect things from other people that they have no idea we want. When we are self-aware, we are more effective in communicating our needs to those around us.

Defining Yourself through Purpose

Becoming self-aware and defining who you are is a critical step in your personal and spiritual growth. This task may seem daunting at first, but as you reflect upon your purpose and determine to succeed, you can accomplish the goal.

First, a growth mindset is vital. Growth is something that is always happening or should be happening. If you think about when we were children, our bodies grew with no permission of our own. As we continued to mature, something happened. It was no longer necessary to develop automatically. However, it became something that we had to consistently and intentionally want and need to do. So, what does it mean to grow outside of the physical sense? Grow: to become larger or greater over some time; increase.

When we come to a place where we find ourselves feeling stuck or having a sense of knowing that something needs to change, that is when we must tap into our potential for growth. Often we will have to change our behavior, actions, and words we speak. Other times we will need to change our surroundings, the people we communicate and connect with, or how we think about ourselves. I have reached these peaks many times in my life. In those times, I often found myself in a dark place wondering, *Why am I here?* I felt alone, trapped, and secluded.

In these times, I knew that God was calling me and pulling me in a direction I wasn't yet ready to embrace. I learned over the years that I'll never entirely be ready for where God is leading. The good thing about this is that he will prepare me. You may be thinking that being ready and being prepared are the same. Well, not quite. Being *ready* means "in a suitable state for an activity, action, or situation or easily obtained; in reach."

In contrast, *prepared* means "made ready for use or ready to do or deal with something." The significant difference is that when prepared, I am *made* ready. For example, I could get dressed for the day and be ready to walk out the door, but if I am not prepared with a vehicle to take me where I'm going, it doesn't matter that I'm ready at all. I would need a ride to where I am "ready" to go.

So, what's my point? We may not always be ready for the changes or growth that takes place in our lives, but by God's grace, we've already been prepared. So, there is absolutely no reason why we can't step out on faith and make the required changes in our lives to do the things that have been predestined. Remember, change is inevitable; growth is optional.

When shifting, we should steer clear of getting stuck in the me-too mindset. You may wonder what that is. Well, I'm speaking about the attitude where we see someone whom we admire or have a connection with walking in purpose, and we begin to think, *I can do that same thing too.* The danger of this is that we will start doing what we are gifted in, but not what we have been purposed in. As children of the kingdom, we know and understand that we have been blessed with many gifts. It's essential to be conscious of the season and time we must operate in those gifts.

I can remember a time years ago when I began watching YouTube videos. I would enjoy watching hair and makeup tutorials. After a while of watching, I started thinking I could do that too. It looked relatively simple because I could create hairstyles and do my makeup. However, when I started making my own YouTube videos a few months before writing this book, I realized it wasn't a piece of cake. There was so much more that went into creating videos that I had absolutely no idea. I then remember feeling overwhelmed, defeated, and stuck.

I was always struggling, trying to think of content to create. What was happening? Before I started creating content, I realized that I needed to know *why* I was creating content. What was my purpose?

Eventually, I decided to give it a break until I knew for sure what I should be doing in that season with that channel. When we get caught up in a me-too mindset, it pushes us further from our destined goal and distracts us from doing what we were put on earth to do. My goal is to help you move past those distractions that take you off course and create a divide between you and your destiny. What I want you to do is think long and hard about your goals, seek God for guidance and direction through prayer, and journal the answers you get. These few steps will equip you for success and the ability to "go and grow." My purpose in telling my story is to inspire you to believe that you can rise above any circumstance and live a destined life of purpose.

Second, to live a life of purpose, we must start with our words because words have power. They can make or break us. It's your job to determine which one it will be, and it starts with what you are speaking. I ran across two words that invaded my heart; as I began to meditate on them, I gained so much clarity. Those two words were *weight* and *wait*. Weight, in essence, is a system of units for heaviness. My mind began to wander, thinking of carrying burdens, worries, hurt, anger, and unforgiveness. If you find yourself walking in the effect of any of these words (like I have plenty of times gone past), right now is your opportunity to speak.

Speak the Word to those circumstances and your emotions:

> FOR CARRYING BURDENS: God's Word says to cast your "anxieties upon him for he cares for you" (The Holy Bible, English Standard Version, 2001, 1 Peter 5:7), and "For my yoke is easy, and my burden is light" (The Holy Bible, English Standard Version, 2001, Matthew 11:30).

> WORRIES: God's Word says, "Do not be anxious about anything, but in everything by prayer and supplication with thanksgiving let your

requests be made known to God. And the peace of God, which surpasses all understanding, will guard your hearts and your minds in Christ Jesus" (The Holy Bible, English Standard Version, 2001, Philippians 4:6–7).

HURT: God's Word says He is the father of compassion and the God of all comfort. He comforts us in all our troubles so that we can comfort those in any trouble with the comfort we receive from him (The Holy Bible, English Standard Version, 2001, 2 Corinthians 1:3).

ANGER: God's Word says, "A soft answer turns away wrath, but a harsh word stirs up anger" (The Holy Bible, English Standard Version, 2001, Proverbs 15:1).

UNFORGIVENESS: God's Word says, "Pride goes before destruction and a haughty spirit before a fall" (The Holy Bible, English Standard Version, 2001, Proverbs 16:18).

We can meditate on these Scriptures and speak life into our circumstances rather than struggle with the weight of life.

The other word, *wait*, means "staying where one is or delaying action until a particular time or until something else happens. Also used to indicate that one is eagerly impatient to do something or for something to happen." When I meditated on *wait*, the words that came to mind were *peace, patience, love*, and *forgiveness*. These words are all the complete opposite of the words that came to mind when I meditated on *weight*. Peace, patience, and love are all considered fruit of the Spirit. Forgiveness is the only one that we must decide to do. Forgiveness does not mean condoning or excusing offenses. It merely means that you choose to let go of deeply rooted negative feelings toward another person. For me, forgiveness helped me to heal and move past negative experiences in my life. Genuinely walking in love helped me to settle in the forgiveness mindset, ultimately freeing myself of my past and pressing forward toward my future.

Third, you must accept the fact that you have the attributes of a victor. A victor is one who gets up when knocked down—and we all know that life has a way of doing that. A victor is one who believes in themselves without a shadow of a doubt. A victor is one who dares to build up their self when others do everything in their power to tear them down. A victor has the courage to fight even when the battle seems like a loss.

I was reminded that I was a victor when I was in prayer one day. The words *release to increase* rose in my spirit. I immediately started sobbing, and I asked the Lord what was meant by these two words.

At that very moment, I looked over at my nightstand and saw a small studded flower-shaped earring that I had recently told my husband I had lost. I was so sad about losing this two-dollar earring from my local beauty supply store, mainly because I liked how they looked in my ears. Weeks prior, I had accepted the fact that it was long gone. As I glanced at the earring, I wondered, *Is this the one I already have?* I opened up my black triangular-shaped glasses case, which is where I would usually keep them. Sure enough, the mate was right there in that box. In that event, this is what was revealed to me: *God is the restorer.* I didn't have to go searching for that which was lost because it was right there in my room when I least expected it.

God is the restorer for a lot of you too. We don't have to stretch ourselves thin, searching for something that we believe we lost. God has a way of revealing, restoring, and even replacing all things to us in due season and time. The only thing we need to do is release it to increase. Release those things that are not producing good fruit or outcomes in our lives and grow in areas that God is prompting and moving us to. Growing could mean releasing anger, bitterness, hurt, shame, or defeat. It could also mean increasing in love, peace, and patience, which opens up the door for victory. You deserve victory in your thought life, family life, financial life, and any other area you can imagine. You are a victor, and I believe you're equipped to do everything you're called to do. Do you?

Fruit of the Spirit: Poems

I have mentioned the fruit of the Spirit and how growing can mean developing this fruit spoken about in Galatians 5:22–23. Meditating on these characteristics that develop as we grow in the Holy Spirit was so meaningful to me that I recorded some of my meditations in poetry and prose. I encourage you to read each of the meditations on a different day, allowing time for the words to get down deep in your spirit and promote growth.

LOVE

What is Love? I imagine with ears,
Love would hear the loud cries of many silent tears.
Because love is a gift of many things,
I wonder, with hands, what it would bring.
Love: it's a comforting hug that a mother gives,
It's a protective fist that a father lifts,
And it's the blessing of an infant, which is an ultimate gift.
Love touches the very depths of one's heart and soul.
Yes, love is a gift of many things in life;
It can be shown by a simple kiss on the forehead of a wife.
Love erases all doubts and any present fears,
And if it could speak, I'm sure it would say,
"Yes, I hear you because I care in a special way."
Love is a gift of many things far, wide, above, and beneath;
It conquers all and rebukes defeat.
Love is the peace that guides all our steps
And is always a constant help.
After all, love is a gift of many things,
For it is seen and unseen.

PEACE

Peace comes like a silent sound;
Even when you can't hear it, you know it's around.

79

Peace is the tap on your shoulder that was never there.
It comes to offer comfort in times of despair;
It's the wind that blows past your ear,
But yet and still, you have no fear.
Yes, peace comes like a silent sound;
Even when you can't see it, you know it's around;
The stab in the back from a dearest friend,
Although it hurts, peace allows you to cope.
The hurt isn't allowed to penetrate your being,
And with no scars to be seen,
Peace has intervened.
Peace is perseverance through the pain of life experiences.
Yes, peace comes like a silent sound;
Even when you can't touch it, you know it's around.
It's the love that surpasses all understanding
And will never become too demanding.
Peace can be a moment in time,
Or it may last forever in your mind.
Peace happens to be a miracle to some,
And once received, Victory shall be won.

FAITHFULNESS

Faithfulness, what can I say about you?
Even in doubt, you still remain true,
And there is never a dull moment with you.
Faithfulness is walking without wavering;
It's praying without ceasing and being broken but still standing.
So again, faithfulness, what can I say about you?
Even in doubt, you still remain true,
And there is never a dull moment with you.
Faith is not seeing but still believing;
It's light shining through the darkness,
And the truth out living a lie.
Faithfulness, indeed, you are set apart;
However, you must always begin in the heart.
Nothing about you is fully shown,
But somehow you still manage to make your presence known.
Faithfulness, if you had a motto, I bet it would be:
Watch, wait, listen, and then there's me.

JOY

Joy comes in the morning, and it stays through the night.
It finds its purpose and shines its light.
Don't underestimate it because it's a sure delight;
Nothing can stand against its powerful might.
Joy is healthy and free,

And I accept that it lives through me.
When it's allowed to captivate you, there's no turning back,
It always remains true, and that's a fact.
God shows us his love and then gives us his peace;
Our faith is grown like a mustard seed,
And in turn, joy proceeds.

LONGSUFFERING

Longsuffering is a test of patience
That provokes endless power.
Endure injustices contentedly, we should
And know that its equipment is for the greater good.
Without complaining, we become like Christ
When he shed his blood and gave his life.

GENTLENESS

Gentleness is the path that we all must take
To meet the needs of others without seeming fake.
Indeed, gentleness is the test of one's true self.
Its calming demeanor resonates from the heart,
And once established, goodness will sprout.

Shame-Less

The experiences shared were life lessons that taught me how to identify who I am and who I want to be. I was often unsure of myself and felt intimidated by the things I didn't know and the answers I was still seeking. Some of my decisions haven't always resulted in the best outcome, which left room for me to become bitter, angry, and dissatisfied with life. However, each time I went through a challenging experience, I knew that embracing a negative mindset would not benefit my growth potential.

I started making intentional efforts to feel each emotion and thought and to tackle them head-on. I also decided that someone who hurt me needed to know the emotion I felt, so I shared it with them. I have been in situations where people would tell me what someone else had done to them, and when I would ask if they had shared it with the individual, their answer would be no. I believe this is a massive mistake that many of us often make. It is difficult to resolve a situation with someone who doesn't know that it negatively impacted you. When we don't allow ourselves to experience our true feelings in their entirety, we miss out on the opportunity to become our best selves.

Thus far, through my experiences, I have become mindful of how I speak toward myself and others. I have learned that it is not always necessary to be right but to become open to others' perspectives. I also have learned that no matter how well other people may see you, it doesn't matter if you don't see the positive in yourself. I know there are so many things I have yet to learn about who I am and how I can become a better wife, mother, daughter, sister, friend, educator, and overall better person. I'm excited about the next phase of the journey that awaits me, and I can honestly say I have become one without shame. I like to call this "shame-less."

Here are three ways you can become shame-less too:

• Forgive yourself for thoughts, feelings, and actions from your past self. Understand that you can only do better when you know better.

• Have compassion for yourself. Realize that we all make mistakes, suffer, and have weaknesses. Remind yourself that you are not alone even if you feel like you are.

• Be accountable. Accountability requires accepting your part in a situation and identifying and acknowledging the pain or hurt, past and current.

Destiny

This is how destiny looks to me:

    Determining your goals

    Evolving into who you are called to be

    Seeking first the kingdom of God and all His righteousness

    Trusting in the Lord with all your heart

    Imagining the best for your life

    Nourishing your growth

    Yielding to the Holy Spirit

Destiny

Journal Your Progress/Process

DATE:

GOAL:

PRAYER:

ANSWER:

*I've included sample journal pages for you to begin your journey.
I encourage you to continue this process in a journal of your own.
I'm praying for you and I want you to remember; you are
DESTINED.*

Journal Your Progress/Process

DATE:

GOAL:

PRAYER:

ANSWER:

*I've included sample journal pages for you to begin your journey.
I encourage you to continue this process in a journal of your own.
I'm praying for you and I want you to remember; you are
DESTINED.*

www.ingramcontent.com/pod-product-compliance
Lightning Source LLC
Chambersburg PA
CBHW070124100426
42744CB00010B/1916